SCHOLASTIC

Building Essential Writing Skills

GRADE 3

New York • Toronto • London • Auckland • Sydney
Mexico City • New Delhi • Hong Kong • Buenos Aires

Writers: Chris Bennett, Immacula Rhodes
Editors: Maria L. Chang, Christy Miller
Cover design: Tannaz Fassihi; Cover art: Eefje Kuijl
Interior design: Shekhar Kapur; Interior art: QBS Learning
Produced with QBS Learning

ISBN: 978-0-545-85041-4
Copyright © 2017 by Scholastic Inc.
All rights reserved.
Printed in the U.S.A.
First printing, January 2017.

1 2 3 4 5 6 7 8 9 10   40   25 24 23 22 21 20 19 18 17

Table of Contents

Table of Contents

Introduction

Help students master key writing skills with these standards-based activities designed to help them become successful writers. The fun, engaging reproducible pages are grouped into lesson packets that provide targeted practice in writing sentences, organizing paragraphs, prewriting, drafting different types of texts, reviewing and improving writing, and revising and editing. Use the lesson to introduce the skills in each packet, then have students complete the pages to reinforce the lesson. As they work through the packets, students learn and practice important skills and concepts, such as types of sentences, capitalization and punctuation, grammar, word choice, developing and organizing ideas, researching, sequencing, adding details, and much more.

These versatile, ready-to-use practice pages can be used in many other ways:

- Select an activity page for use as a "do now" activity to help get students settled first thing in the morning. Simply stack copies of the page on a table for students to pick up as they enter the room. Then allow a specific amount of time, such as five minutes, for them to complete the activity.

- Preview the day's lesson with a related skills page. You can use the activity to find out what students already know about the topic.

- Alternatively, you can use an activity page to review a previously learned lesson, assess what students have learned, and determine where they need further instruction.

- Assign a skills page for students to complete independently, with a partner, in small groups, or for homework.

An answer key is provided at the back of the book so you can review answers with students. In doing so, you provide opportunities to discuss, reinforce, or extend skills to other lessons. Students can also share their responses and strategies in small groups. This collaboration will enable them to deepen their understanding or clarify any misunderstandings they may have about the skill or the writing process.

Meeting the Standards

The activities in this book meet the following standards for Grade 3.

Writing

Students will:

- Write opinion pieces on topics or texts, supporting a point of view with reasons.
- Introduce the topic or text they are writing about, state an opinion, and create an organizational structure that lists reasons.
- Provide reasons that support the opinion.
- Use linking words and phrases (e.g., *because, therefore, since, for example*) to connect opinion and reasons.
- Provide a concluding statement or section.
- Write informative/explanatory texts to examine a topic and convey ideas and information clearly.
- Introduce a topic and group related information together; include illustrations when useful to aiding comprehension.
- Develop the topic with facts, definitions, and details.
- Use linking words and phrases (e.g., *also, another, and, more, but*) to connect ideas within categories of information.
- Provide a concluding statement or section.
- Write narratives to develop real or imagined experiences or events, using effective technique, descriptive details, and clear sequences.
- Establish a situation and introduce a narrator and/or characters; organize an event sequence that unfolds naturally.
- Use dialogue and descriptions of actions, thoughts, and feelings to develop experiences and events or show the response of characters to situations.
- Use temporal words and phrases to signal event order.
- Provide a sense of closure.
- With guidance and support from adults, produce writing in which the development and organization are appropriate to the task and purpose.
- With guidance and support from peers and adults, develop and strengthen writing as needed by planning, revising, and editing.
- Recall information from experiences or gather information from print and digital sources; take brief notes on sources and sort evidence into provided categories.

Language

Students will:

- Explain the function of nouns, pronouns, verbs, adjectives, and adverbs in general and their functions in particular sentences.
- Form and use regular and irregular plural nouns.
- Use abstract nouns (e.g., *childhood*).
- Form and use regular and irregular verbs.
- Form and use the simple verb tenses.
- Ensure subject-verb and pronoun-antecedent agreement.
- Produce simple, compound, and complex sentences.
- Use commas and quotation marks in dialogue.
- Consult reference materials, including beginning dictionaries, as needed to check spelling.
- Choose words and phrases for effect.
- Identify and use shades of meaning.

Lesson 1: Strong Sentences

Objective
Students will review sentence structure and types of sentences. They will write simple, complex, and compound sentences.

Standards
• Produce simple, compound, and complex sentences.
• Use correct capitalization and punctuation, including in dialogue.

What You Need
Copies of this packet for each student; whiteboard and markers

What to Do

1. Write a few sentences on the board. Read the sentences aloud. Use them to review the basics of sentences, pointing out the capital letter at the beginning and the punctuation at the end of each sentence.

2. Explain that sentences have a subject and a verb. The **subject** is who or what the sentence is about, and the **verb** tells the action. Have volunteers come to the board to draw a box around the subject of the sentences or underline the verbs. Distribute copies of "The Rabbit" (page 8) for students to complete.

3. Use "My Favorite Bird" (page 9) to review the four types of sentences: declarative, interrogative, imperative, and exclamatory. Remind students that a declarative sentence is a statement, an interrogative sentence asks a question, an imperative gives a command, and an exclamatory sentence expresses a strong feeling.

4. Distribute copies of "Sunny Places," "The Safari Park," and "Tingly Feet" (pages 10–12) and use them to review capitalization and punctuation.

5. Use "Weather on Mars" (page 13) to give students practice in recognizing subject-verb and pronoun-antecedent agreement.

6. To help students understand the difference between the kinds of sentences, write an example of a simple, complex, and compound sentence on the board. Demonstrate how to add a phrase to a simple sentence to create a complex sentence and how to combine two simple sentences to make a compound sentence. Then have students complete "Weather Details," "Lightning Speed," and "Storm Chasers" (pages 14–16).

Name: _____   Date: _____

 A **sentence** is a group of words that tells a complete thought. A sentence includes a subject, which tells who or what the sentence is about. It also includes a verb, which tells what happened.

The Rabbit

Read the short story. Then complete the activities below.

(**1**) A rabbit hopped into Janet's backyard. (**2**) It sprang from one end of the yard to the other. (**3**) Suddenly, the rabbit stopped.

1. Circle the subject in sentence 1.

2. Circle *It* in sentence 2. This pronoun is the subject. What does the pronoun refer to?

It → _____

3. Underline the verb in sentence 2.

4. What is the subject in sentence 3? Write it in the oval. Then write the verb on the line.

 _____

5. Write a sentence to tell why the rabbit stopped. Include a subject and verb in your sentence.

_____

There are four types of sentences. A **declarative** sentence makes a statement. An **imperative** sentence gives a command. An **interrogative** sentence asks a question. And an **exclamatory** sentence expresses a strong feeling, like "I know the four sentence types!"

My Favorite Bird

Read this conversation. Then identify the types of sentences.

Hector: The roadrunner is my favorite bird.

Jimbo: You must be joking! A roadrunner can hardly fly.

Hector: That's what makes it special.

Jimbo: It's special because it can't fly? Tell me why.

Hector: It can run so fast, it doesn't need to fly.

> **What kind of sentence is *this*?**

1. Find the imperative sentence in the conversation. Write it on line.

_____

2. Find the exclamatory sentence in the conversation. Write it on the line.

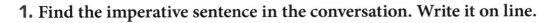

3. Find the interrogative sentence. Write it on the line.

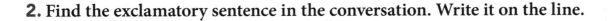

4. How many declarative sentences are in the conversation?

    a. 1   **b.** 2   **c.** 3   **d.** 4

Name: _____   Date: _____

Capitalize the first letter in proper nouns, including names, places, months, and days of the week.

Sunny Places

Read the passage. Draw three lines under each letter that should be capitalized. Example: florida

(**1**) Florida is called the sunshine state, but maybe this should be arizona's nickname. (**2**) Arizona is, in fact, the sunniest state in the united states. (**3**) And yuma, arizona, is the sunniest city. (**4**) The sun shines there 90 percent of the time. (**5**) In june, it shines 97 percent of the time. (**6**) However, st. petersburg, florida, holds the record for the most clear days in a row. (**7**) The sun came out every day there from february 9, 1967, to march 17, 1969. (**8**) That's more than two years of soaking up rays!

Do you know the way to Arizona?

Follow the sun.

Now write the words that should be capitalized in each sentence.

1._____   5._____

2._____   6._____

3._____   7._____

4._____   8._____

Always capitalize the first word in a sentence and proper names, such as the name of a person or place. Punctuate the end of a sentence. Use commas to separate items in a series.

The Safari Park

Read each sentence. Find the capitalization and punctuation mistakes. Rewrite the sentences correctly.

1. My friend enrique visited springfield safari park last week. Animals from africa roam freely around the park.

_____

_____

2. Enrique drove his car through the park? he said an ostrich stuck its head into the sunroof

_____

_____

3. A zebra llama and warthog also came right up to his car. enrique enjoyed seeing so many animals up close

_____

_____

4. would you like to visit a safari park! what animals would you hope to see.

_____

_____

Dialogue helps to bring characters to life. Use quotation marks at the beginning and end of what a characters says.

Tingly Feet

Use a comma to separate a quote from who says it. The comma goes before the ending quotation mark.	*"I could use a superhero right now," said Jackie.*
Do not use a comma if the quote ends with an exclamation point or question mark.	*"I think I see one!" cried Juanita.*

Underline each sentence with incorrect punctuation. Rewrite the sentences below.

1. "What's the matter" asked Yadier. "You look a little strange."

_____

2. "I'm not sure" replied Jasper. "I rubbed this old coin, and now my feet feel tingly."

_____

3. Tingly, like your foot is asleep?

_____

4. "No, tingly like my feet are ready to run 200 miles a minute".

_____

5. Wow! That's a pretty good tingle, said Yadier.

_____

Building Essential Writing Skills: Grade 3 © Scholastic Inc.

> Use a singular verb with a singular subject and a plural verb with a plural subject.
> For example: *The dog is tired. The dogs are tired.*
> When using a pronoun, make sure it matches the subject.
> For example: *The dog shakes when it gets wet.*

Weather on Mars

Read the passage. Circle the correct verb for each sentence.

What *(is/are)* the weather like on Mars? For one thing, it *(is/are)* very dry. No rain *(fall/falls)*. In the summer at noon, temperatures *(is/are)* comfortable. A high of 68 degrees *(have/has)* been recorded at the planet's equator. But temperatures *(plunge/plunges)* at night all over Mars. The equator *(is/are)* 170 degrees colder after dark. Sometimes dust devils and dust storms *(develop/develops)* on Mars. When this happens, the dust *(stay/stays)* in the air for months.

Write the correct pronoun for each sentence.

1. The weather can be warm on Mars, but _____ *(it/that)* gets cold at night.

2. People who want to live on Mars know _____ *(them/they)* have a long wait.

3. Maria jumped up and down when _____ *(she/her)* won the Mars Scholar award.

4. Scientists want to send another probe to Mars so _____ *(it/they)* can study the planet some more.

Add **details** to sentences to provide more information and to make them more interesting. For example: *The boy wrote notes. The curious boy wrote a page full of notes.*

Weather Details

Rewrite each simple sentence.
Add details that make it more interesting.

1. Simple sentence: The snow falls.

_____

_____

2. Simple sentence: We heard thunder.

_____

_____

3. Now look out your window. Write about the weather you see.
   Include details in your sentences.

_____

_____

_____

_____

Building Essential Writing Skills: Grade 3 © Scholastic Inc.

Name: _____ Date: _____

 A **complex sentence** includes more information about the main idea of a sentence. It includes parts that cannot stand alone.

Lightning Speed

Read the passage. Then complete the activities below.

Here is an easy way to tell how far away lightning is from you. When you are near a thunderstorm, watch for a flash of lightning. Then count the number of seconds until a crack of thunder follows it. Divide that number by 5. This number tells you how many miles away you are from the lightning strike. If you counted 40 seconds, then the lightning struck 8 miles away. Take cover if the time between the lightning and thunder is 30 seconds or less. This means the lightning is about 6 miles away.

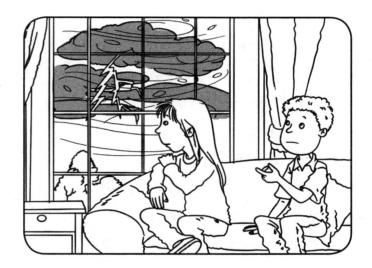

Read each sentence below. Then add to the sentence. Choose the clause that gives more information.

1. If you counted 40 seconds, then the lightning struck 8 miles away,

    a. since you know how to do math.

    b. because 40 divided by 5 is 8.

    c. if you have a calculator.

2. This means the lightning is about 6 miles away,

    a. and that's less than 10 miles away.

    b. but you don't need to worry.

    c. which is closer than you think.

Name: _____ Date: _____

Storm Chasers

Read the passage. Then complete the activities below.

(**1**) Storm chasers follow stormy weather in cars as it happens. (**2**) What they see in the dark skies can help save lives. (**3**) They pass information on to weather services. (**4**) These services pass it on to you. (**5**) Storm chasers also collect information that can help predict future storms. (**6**) They have an important job, but they must do it safely. (**7**) It is impossible to know exactly what will happen inside a thunderstorm. (**8**) Storm chasers may see a tornado and follow its path. (**9**) They don't want to be *in* the tornado's path.

Sentence 6 is a compound sentence. Write the two sentences that make up this compound sentence.

1. _____

2. _____

Form a compound sentence with each pair of sentences. Use a comma and conjunction, such as *and, but,* or *or.* (Hint: Use sentence 6 as a model.)

3. Sentences 3 and 4: _____

_____

4. Sentences 8 and 9: _____

_____

Building Essential Writing Skills: Grade 3 © Scholastic Inc.

Lesson 2: Powerful Paragraphs

Objective
Students will identify the parts of a paragraph (introduction, body, and conclusion) and write appropriately structured texts for different types of writing.

Standards
Write opinion, informative, and narrative pieces that include an introduction, a body of text that has been developed appropriately for the type of writing, and a concluding statement or section.

What You Need
Copies of this packet for each student; whiteboard and markers

What to Do
1. Write or display the passage from "The Gray Wolf" (page 18) on the board. Distribute copies of the page to students. Read the paragraph aloud to students. Explain that the first sentence is the **introduction**. It tells the main idea of the paragraph, or what the paragraph is about. Invite a student to come to the board and underline the introduction. Talk about the importance of a strong introduction, then have students complete the page. Use "Ice From the Sky" (page 19) to give further practice in writing introductions.

2. Explain that the **conclusion** comes at the end of a passage. The concluding statement (or section) usually repeats the introduction, but in a different way. Distribute "A Fast Learner" (page 20) and "Sticky Weather" (page 21) to reinforce understanding of writing conclusions.

3. Point out that the **body** of the paragraph is made up of the sentences between the introduction and conclusion. The body provides more information about the topic. In an opinion text, the body provides reasons that support the opinion. In an informative text, it features facts and details about the topic. The body of a narrative text includes story elements, such as characters, a setting, and a plot, and presents events of the story in a logical order. Use "Sea Foam" (page 22) and "A Magical Dance" (page 23) to reinforce writing a body that helps make a strong paragraph.

When writing a paragraph, use the **introduction** to present the topic and grab the reader's attention. You might use a question, a quote, or a surprising fact as your first sentence.

The Gray Wolf

Read the passage. Then complete the activities below.

The gray wolf needs to be rescued again. In 1974, there were almost no gray wolves in the United States. Hunters had killed them. Then gray wolves were brought into Yellowstone Park in the 1990s. New laws protected the wolves so no one could kill them. There are now gray wolves in several states. But now they can be hunted again. The gray wolf needs to be protected like before, or it will be wiped out once more.

1. **A good introduction presents the topic and grabs the reader's attention. Why is this important?**

   a. The reader will have all the information needed.

   b. The reader will be interested and want to read on.

   c. The reader can stop reading.

   d. The reader can move on to the last sentence.

2. **Underline the introduction in the paragraph above. Then write your own introduction. Try to make it stronger than the current one.** (Hint: You might use a question, exclamation, or interesting fact.)

   _____

   _____

Building Essential Writing Skills: Grade 3 © Scholastic Inc.

When writing your introduction, ask yourself: *If I were the reader, would my introduction make me want to read on?*

Ice From the Sky

Read the passage. Then complete the activities below.

Like lightning and tornadoes, hail can be a dangerous part of a thunderstorm. These chunks of ice falling from the sky can damage homes, cars, and other properties. They can also injure people. The biggest hailstone on record fell in South Dakota in 2010. It was 8 inches in diameter and weighed about 2 pounds. Luckily, no one was hurt during that storm.

1. Underline the introduction in the paragraph. Circle the main idea of that sentence.

2. What does the introduction tell the reader?
   a. It tells the reader that the topic is tornadoes.
   b. It tells the reader that the topic is hail.
   c. It tells the reader that the topic is lightning.
   d. It tells the reader not to worry about hail.

3. Write your own introduction for the paragraph. (Hint: You might use a question, exclamation, or interesting fact.)

_____

_____

Name: _____ Date: _____

A Fast Learner

Read the passage. Then complete the activities below.

I think my dog is smarter than my sister. My sister, Helene, is 1 year old, and she doesn't know anything. My dog, Charley, is 6 months old, and he gets things right. He sleeps at the right time. He barks when he should. And he eats exactly when his food is given to him. My sister doesn't do any of these things. She wakes up in the middle of the night. She cries for no reason. She never seems interested in eating. She just mashes it all over her face!

1. **Which sentence would make the best conclusion for the paragraph?**
   a. I'm pretty sure a dog's brain grows faster than a human's.
   b. My dog usually doesn't eat my homework.
   c. I've got a sister for sale.
   d. My dog hunts squirrels and rabbits.

2. Underline the introduction. Then write your own conclusion to the paragraph. Try to restate the introduction in a new way.

_____

_____

Building Essential Writing Skills: Grade 3 © Scholastic Inc.

A conclusion should sum up the main idea of a paragraph. The conclusion can state a fact, ask a question, or give an opinion.

Sticky Weather

Read the passage. Then complete the activities below.

On a hot and very humid day, the air makes you feel sticky and sweaty. Humidity is a measure of water vapor in the air. But for most people, it's just a measure of how uncomfortable they are outside. A very humid day can be a good thing, though. Believe it or not, high humidity can make you sing better. It's also good for your skin. And higher humidity in the winter can help protect you from a cold or the flu. Also, plants thrive in high humidity.

1. What is the main idea of the paragraph?

_____

_____

2. Write your own conclusion to the paragraph. Try to sum up the main idea.

_____

_____

3. Write another conclusion to the paragraph. Include your opinion in the sentence.

_____

_____

The **body** of a paragraph gives details or more information about the main idea.
The body is made up of sentences that come between the introduction and conclusion.

Sea Foam

**Read the passage. Underline the introduction.
Circle the conclusion.**

Sometimes the ocean can be foamy like a bubble bath. In Australia, sea foam as high as 6 feet can wash ashore. It can cover cars and block street signs. How does sea foam form? When algae in the ocean breaks down, it creates air bubbles. Rough seas and high winds stir up the air bubbles until foam appears. Another event that can create this sea foam is rain. Heavy rains near shore can wash nutrients from soil into the ocean. This can cause the algae to produce foam. It might be fun to swim in an ocean-size bathtub of foam, but it won't make you clean!

1. What is the main idea of the paragraph?

_____

_____

2. Write three things that the body of the paragraph tells you.

_____

_____

_____

Building Essential Writing Skills: Grade 3 © Scholastic Inc.

A story follows a logical **sequence**. In a short story, the body includes sentences that tell the events in the order that they happen.

A Magical Dance

Read the first part of the short story.

Nadia wanted so badly to be the fairy princess at her ballet recital. But every time she tried to do a spin, she fell. "Don't worry," said her ballet teacher. "You can be fairy princess next year."

Now read the sentences that belong to the body. Put them in the correct order. Use numbers 1 to 5.

_____ Then she gave Nadia a new pair of purple toe shoes.

_____ Afterwards, her ballet teacher asked Nadia to be fairy princess at this year's recital.

_____ The next day at dance class, Nadia spun like a tornado in her new shoes.

_____ One day, a mysterious old ballerina showed up at the school.

_____ When she finally stopped spinning, everyone in class clapped wildly.

Write a conclusion to the story.

_____

_____

_____

Lesson 3: Getting Ready to Write

Objective
Students will choose a topic, brainstorm, and gather and organize information for different types of writing.

Standards
• Develop and strengthen writing as needed by planning, revising, and editing.
• Produce writing in which the development and organization are appropriate to the task and purpose for writing (opinion, informative/explanatory, or narrative text).

What You Need
Copies of this packet for each student; whiteboard and markers

What to Do

1. Draw or display the organizer from "Animal Choices" (page 25) on the board. Distribute copies of the page to students. Explain that an organizer can help them select a topic for an opinion text. Point out the subject at the center of the organizer (Animals) and review the headings in the ovals. Help students brainstorm another heading to add to the organizer. Demonstrate how to fill in a few animals that fit each category. Then have students complete the rest of their organizer on their own.

2. Distribute copies of "The Case for Zoos" (page 26). Explain that this page can be used to jot down reasons for an opinion before writing an opinion text. Review the parts of the organizer and how to use it. Then have students complete it on their own. Use "The Best Pet" (page 27) to give students additional practice in using an organizer to prepare for writing an opinion piece.

3. Use "Wet Weather," "Hot Places," and "Historic Snowfall" (pages 28–30) to help students practice using organizers to choose a topic, brainstorm ideas, and gather facts and information for an informative text. Have them complete "It's a Monsoon!" (page 31) to learn about resources they can use when doing research for their writing.

4. Have students complete "My Superhero," "My Story Ideas," and "Mr. Freeze-It" (pages 32–34) to organize their ideas for narrative texts. Review and explain what the story elements of character, plot, and setting are, and talk about the importance of presenting events in a logical sequence.

5. Set students' organizers aside. Explain that they might want to use some of them when writing a draft during Lesson 4.

Name: _____ Date: _____

> In **opinion writing**, you state what you think or feel about a topic and give reasons why. Using an organizer can help you select a topic for an opinion text.

Animal Choices

Imagine you will write an opinion text about animals.
Use the organizer to help you choose a topic.

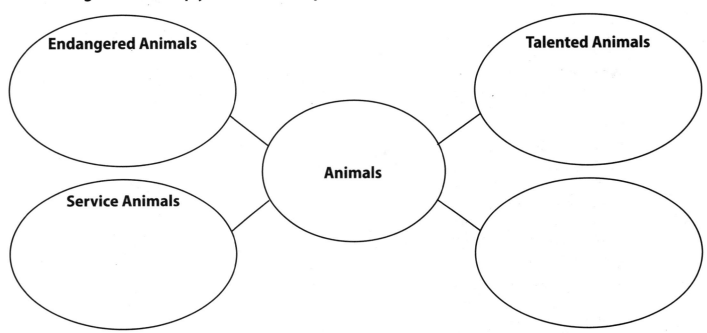

Endangered Animals

Talented Animals

Animals

Service Animals

1. Which heading would be a good topic to add to the organizer?
Write your choice in the empty section of the organizer.

   a. Plants and Animals   **c.** Camouflaged Animals

   b. Animal Books   **d.** Animal Homes

2. Read the category in each outer oval of the organizer. Fill in a few animals that fit that category.

3. Use the information on the organizer to choose a topic. Write an opinion statement about your topic.

_____

_____

Name: _____   Date: _____

To prepare for writing an opinion text, you can use an organizer to brainstorm reasons that support your opinion.

The Case for Zoos

Read the opinion and reasons in the organizer. Then complete the activities below.

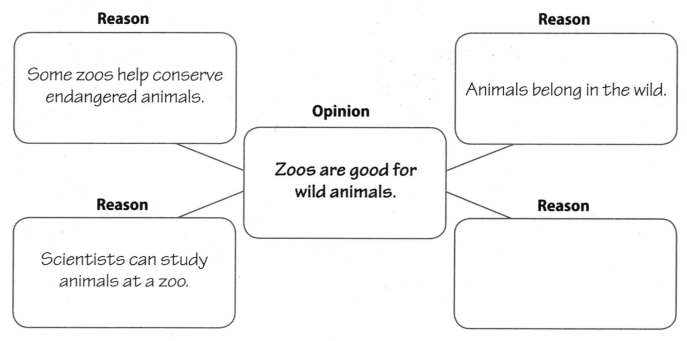

Reason

Some zoos help conserve endangered animals.

Opinion

Zoos are good for wild animals.

Reason

Animals belong in the wild.

Reason

Scientists can study animals at a zoo.

Reason

1. **Which of the following is a reason that supports the opinion? Write your choice in the empty section of the organizer.**
   a. Every state in the U.S. has some kind of zoo.
   b. The reptile house is my favorite place at the zoo.
   c. Zoos provide for the needs of wild animals.
   d. The San Diego Zoo has giant pandas.

2. **Which reason in the organizer does not support the opinion? Cross it out.**

3. **Do some research to find an appropriate reason to replace the one you crossed out. Write your reason below.**

_____

_____

Building Essential Writing Skills: Grade 3 © Scholastic Inc.

Name: _____   Date: _____

> Organize your opinion writing by including support for each of your reasons.

The Best Pet

Complete the activities below. Use the organizer to help you.

Opinion	Dogs are better pets than cats.
Reason 1	Dogs make better companions.
Reason 2	Dogs help keep your home and family safe.
Reason 3	It's good fun and good exercise to walk a dog.
Reason 4	

1. Think of another reason that supports the opinion in the organizer. Write your reason in the empty box.

2. Which sentence best supports Reason 1?
   a. Dogs don't get sick very often.
   b. Dogs will bark at your neighbors.
   c. Dogs love to be around people and help them.
   d. Dogs will clean your kitchen by eating the food you leave behind.

3. Write a sentence that supports each reason.

Reason 2: _____

Reason 3: _____

Reason 4: _____

Building Essential Writing Skills: Grade 3 © Scholastic Inc.

Name: _____   Date: _____

Wet Weather

Imagine you have an assignment to write an informative text related to wet weather. Use the organizer to help you choose a topic.

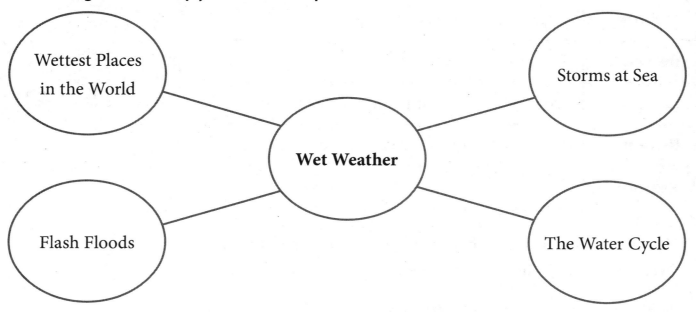

1. Which topic in the organizer would be a good choice if you wanted to write about shipwrecks. Underline it.

2. Which topic would be a good choice if you wanted to write about cities that get the most rain. Draw a rectangle around it.

3. Which of the following would be a good topic if you were interested in the science of storms? Circle your choice.
   a. A Thunderstorm Is Born
   b. Collecting Rainwater
   c. How to Drive in Wet Weather
   d. The 1900 Galveston Hurricane

When preparing to write an informational text, ask yourself what you would like to know about your topic. Then go find the answers. Take notes on facts, definitions, and other details.

Hot Places

Complete the activities below.
Use this outline to help you.

Topic	Hot Places
Subtopics	• Hottest place in the U.S. • Record-setting temperatures • Deserts

1. **Look at the subtopics in the outline. Which question could you ask yourself about one of the subtopics?**

   a. How hot is the sun?

   b. How does a cactus survive the desert heat?

   c. What creatures live in the deep waters of Antarctica?

   d. Is melted rock below the Earth's crust?

2. **What could you ask yourself about the hottest place in the U.S.? Write your question.**

   _____

   _____

3. **What could you ask yourself about record-setting temperatures? Write your question.**

   _____

   _____

Building Essential Writing Skills: Grade 3 © Scholastic Inc.

Name: _____ Date: _____

Historic Snowfall

Complete the activities below.
Use the organizer to help you.

Topic: The 2015 record snowfall in Boston, Massachusetts	
Questions	**Answers**
What conditions create a snowfall?	
How much snow fell?	At least twice as much snow as normal • Boston, MA, 78.5 inches (27.4 normal) • Worcester, MA, 92.1 inches (40.6 normal)
How did the snow affect the area?	Schools and business closed. Snow had to be moved to empty lots.

1. **Which detail answers the first question in the organizer?**
   a. Snowflakes are crystal hexagons.
   b. Antarctica is cold but has little snow.
   c. Temperatures below freezing may build up a snow pack.
   d. Snow forms at or below 0°C (32°F) when moisture is in the air.

2. **What other question could you ask about the record snowfall? Write it under "Questions" in the organizer.**

3. **Do some research to find an answer to your question. Write what you learned under "Answers" in the organizer.**

Name: _____   Date: _____

It's a Monsoon!

Ann is writing an informative text on monsoons. Help her by answering the questions below. Use the words in the box.

| atlas | encyclopedia | dictionary | weather website |

1. Which resource can Ann use to find a definition of *monsoon*?

_____

2. Which resource can she use to learn about why monsoons occur?

_____

3. Which resource would give Ann information about current monsoon weather conditions?

_____

4. Which resource can help her locate places in the world that are affected by monsoons?

_____

Name: _____ Date: _____

Sometimes an idea about a character can become the basis for a **narrative text**, or story. You can use an organizer to write down your ideas about a character.

My Superhero

This organizer shows a few qualities of a superhero character you might write about. Use the organizer to complete the activities below.

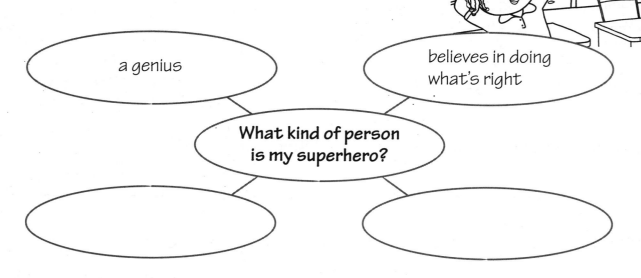

1. Think of two more qualities your superhero might have. Write each quality in an empty oval of the organizer.

2. List two super powers your superhero could have.

_____

_____

3. Some things your superhero might do are listed below. Add one more thing to the list.
My superhero can:

• solve a mystery from the past that will change a future event

• stop a bad guy from stealing electricity

• become an animal to help characters in the animal world

• _____

Building Essential Writing Skills: Grade 3 © Scholastic Inc.

Name: _____   Date: _____

Sometimes an idea about a place or something that happens (real or make-believe) becomes the basis for a narrative text, or story. Use an organizer to write down ideas about your story.

My Story Ideas

Think about a story you would like to tell. You can use the picture to help you come up with an idea. Write your ideas in the organizer.

Characters
(Who will the story be about?)

Setting
(Where and when will the story take place?)

My Story
(What is the main idea of the story?)

Plot
(What are some things that will happen in the story?)

Name: _____ Date: _____

Mr. Freeze-It

These sentences describe events that will be used in a story about a superhero.
Put the sentences in a logical order. Use the numbers 1 to 6.

_____ First, Mr. Freeze-It waved his hand and said, "Freeze!" He used his superpowers to stop all motion.

_____ Finally, he snapped his fingers and commanded, "Unfreeze!"

_____ Jamie and Ellie always made fun of Carmine at school.

_____ Then, Mr. Freeze-It told the frozen children they needed to be nice to one another at all times.

_____ The three children began to move again. From then on, they were the best of friends!

_____ One day, a superhero named Mr. Freeze-It appeared in their class.

1. Circle the sequence and time words in the sentences. How did these words help you understand the order of events?

_____

_____

2. Continue the plot. Write a few sentences about what Mr. Freeze-It will do next.

_____

_____

_____

Lesson 4: Writing for a Purpose

Objective
Students will identify different kinds of writing and set a purpose for writing.

Standards
- Write opinion pieces on topics or texts, supporting a point of view with reasons.
- Write informative/explanatory texts to examine a topic and convey ideas and information clearly.
- Write narratives to develop real or imagined experiences or events, using effective technique, descriptive details, and clear sequences.

What You Need
Copies of this packet for each student; whiteboard and markers

What to Do
1. Tell students that the purpose of writing an **opinion text** is to share what you think or feel about a particular topic. In the text, the writer provides reasons for the opinion and details to support the reasons. Remind students that they can fill out an organizer to brainstorm and organize their ideas before writing and then use their notes to write a draft. Review the basics of an opinion text with "A Home Aquarium" (page 36) and "We Can Be Gazelles" (page 37). Then have students use the "My Favorite Movie Animal" organizer and companion page (pages 38–39) to draft an opinion text.

2. Explain that in an **informative text**, the writer shares facts and information that has been gathered through reading and research. Display "Dust Devils" (page 40) on the board. Distribute copies of the page and review it with students. Have them complete the page to examine how details help explain a topic. Then have students fill out the organizer for "Dangerous Weather" (page 41) and use the information to write a draft on the companion draft-writing page (page 42).

3. Remind students that a **narrative text** tells a story that follows a logical order. A story includes characters, a setting, and a plot and can be real or made up. Distribute "'Green Storm' Norm" (page 43) and "Elvin's Story" (page 44) to help reinforce students' understanding of story elements. Pass out "Fastball Fran" (page 45), discuss the differences in writing from different perspectives, then have students complete the page. Finally, instruct students to fill out the organizer for "The Talking Animal" (page 46) and write their story on the companion draft-writing page (page 47).

4. Invite students to pull out organizers they have previously completed and use them for their drafts. After students edit and revise their text, they can write their final text on a copy of the writing template (page 61).

Name: _____ Date: _____

 When you draft an opinion essay, include details that support your reasons.

A Home Aquarium

Read the reasons and supporting details for having a home aquarium.
Draw a line to match each Supporting Detail to the Reason it supports.

Reasons

1. Watching the fish is relaxing.

2. I can control what is in my aquarium.

3. An aquarium can have tropical fishes from around the world.

Supporting Details

a. My aquarium will have fish I'd never see in lakes or rivers.

b. Studies show that a home aquarium lowers blood pressure.

c. An aquarium is like my own water garden.

Now write a draft that gives the opinion that having a home aquarium is good.
Include reasons for the opinion and details that support those reasons.
(Hint: You can use some of the reasons and supporting details above.)

_____

_____

_____

_____

_____

When writing an argument, the opinion should always be supported by reasons.

We Can Be Gazelles

Read Nina's draft, which tells her opinion about a new nickname for her school team. Then complete the activities below.

The nickname for our school sports team should be Gazelles. A gazelle is one of the fastest land animals. It reaches speeds of 60 miles per hour. It is also smart. When they run, gazelles zigzag and make sharp turns. This helps them avoid predators, like cheetahs and leopards. Gazelles are good sports, too. An adult male does not enter the area of another male. If our team is fast and smart, and our players are good sports, we will have many championship seasons.

1. Write the two sentences in the draft that state Nina's opinions.

_____

_____

2. Write two reasons that support Nina's opinion.

_____

_____

3. What is the main point of Nina's opinion?
   a. If a team uses the nickname "Gazelles," it will win many championships.
   b. Adult male gazelles are scared of other males.
   c. A good nickname for a team is "Gazelles" because they are fast, smart, and good sports.
   d. By using the nickname "Gazelles," a team can avoid predators.

Building Essential Writing Skills: Grade 3 © Scholastic Inc.

Organizer: My Favorite Movie Animal

Complete the sentence in the center of the organizer. Then fill in reasons for your opinion and details to support the reasons.

Reason:

Detail:

Reason:

Detail:

Opinion

My favorite movie animal is

_____.

Reason:

Detail:

Reason:

Detail:

Draft: My Favorite Movie Animal

Write the first draft of your opinion. Use your notes.

_____

_____

_____

_____

_____

_____

_____

_____

_____

_____

_____

_____

Now check your work.

Words	Paragraphs	Punctuation and Grammar
☐ Use linking words to connect ideas.	☐ Write complete sentences.	☐ Use commas in a series.
☐ Use adjectives and adverbs.	☐ Use reasons to support opinions.	☐ Use correct verb tenses.

Name: _____ Date: _____

When you draft an informative/explanatory text, include interesting details from your research that help explain your topic.

Dust Devils

Read Ned's draft about dust devils.
Then complete the activities below.

If you've ever seen a whirl of dust rising in the air, it may have been a dust devil. A dust devil forms when hot air on the ground rises up into cooler air. This makes the air spin and stretch up into a column. Loose dirt on the ground gets sucked up into it. The wind inside a dust devil is not as strong as a tornado, so dust devils almost never cause damage.

1. Circle the introduction of the paragraph. Which sentence could Ned add after the introduction to help explain his topic?

    a. Wind speeds inside a tornado can reach 300 miles per hour.

    b. I've never seen a dust devil.

    c. A dust devil looks like a small tornado and appears on open, flat land.

    d. A tornado happens during a super cell storm.

2. Ned asked himself these questions about dust devils before he began his research. What would *you* like to know about dust devils? Add your questions to the list.

    • How is a dust devil formed?

    • How does a dust devil compare to a tornado?

_____

_____

Building Essential Writing Skills: Grade 3 © Scholastic Inc.

Organizer: Dangerous Weather

Choose a weather event to use as a topic for your informative text. You can choose from the box below or come up with your own. Do some research, then fill in the organizer with facts and details that you learned about your choice. (Hint: Use dictionaries, encyclopedias, books, and websites.)

| flood | dust storm | hurricane |
| thunderstorm | blizzard | heat wave |

What is it?

What causes it?

Weather

What effect does it have?

Draft: Dangerous Weather

Write the first draft of your informative text. Use your notes.

_____

_____

_____

_____

_____

_____

_____

_____

_____

_____

_____

Now check your work.

Words	Paragraphs	Punctuation and Grammar
☐ Use linking words to connect ideas.	☐ Include introduction and conclusion.	☐ Use subject-verb agreement.
☐ Use precise language.	☐ Include interesting facts and details.	☐ Use noun-pronoun agreement.

Name: _____ Date: _____

When writing a story, include details about the characters and setting. The **characters** are who the story is about. The **setting** is the place and time of the story.

"Green Storm" Norm

Read Julia's draft about a boy with green hair.
Then complete the activities below.

A tornado came down in 8-year-old Norman Haskin's backyard in Headwind, Kansas. It sucked him up for a few seconds and spun him around inside. A moment later, Norman was right back in his yard. His little sister, Regina, was in her sandbox. With her mouth wide open, she pointed at Norman's hair. It had turned bright green! It glowed like a magic lamp. Since that day, no tornado has struck the town of Headwind again. When wind and dark clouds come near, Norman just shakes his head of green hair at it. The storm disappears! To everyone in town, "Green Storm" Norm is Headwind's storm-stopping superhero.

1. Who is the main character in Julia's story? _____
   Write some things from the story that you learned about this character.

   _____

   _____

   _____

2. What is the setting for Julia's story? _____
   Write one detail about the setting.

   _____

3. Write another detail about the setting that Julia could use in her story.
   (Hint: It can be about the time or place.)

   _____

Name: _____   Date: _____

 The **plot** of a story is made up of a series of events. The main character of the story usually faces a problem and finds some way to solve it.

Elvin's Story

Draft a story about Elvin playing in a basketball game. Use the following characters, setting, and plot in your story.

Setting: A basketball game

Plot: Elvin's team is behind by one point with 10 seconds left on the clock.

Characters:

Elvin, a 9-year-old boy who is not very good at basketball

Roz, a very good player on Elvin's team

Coach Beale, the basketball coach

_____

_____

_____

_____

_____

_____

_____

Building Essential Writing Skills: Grade 3 © Scholastic Inc.

Name: _____ Date: _____

> A story is usually told from one of two different **points of view**. In **first person**, the main character tells the story using pronouns like *I* and *we*. In **third person**, someone else tells the story using the pronouns *he*, *she*, and *they*.

Fastball Fran

Review the chart about point of view. Then complete the activities below.

Point of View	Pronouns	Example
First person	I, we	*I do not think my phone is working.*
Third person	he, she, they	*She thinks her phone is not working.*

Fastball Fran had just completed her 384th no-hitter. As she signed autographs outside the stadium, an elderly woman came up and congratulated her. "That was an excellent game today," she said.

"Thanks," Fran mumbled without looking up.

"I used to pitch, too," added the woman.

"Really?" Fran said, disbelievingly.

"Yes," replied the woman. "Want to see?"

Fran handed the woman a ball, then walked several feet away. When Fran held up her mitt, the elderly woman threw a fastball, right in the strike zone!

"Wow!" Fran remarked, as she jogged back to the woman. "You're amazing!"

"Thank you," replied the woman. "I used to pitch for the All-American Girls Professional Baseball League. My name is Jean Faut."

Fran's jaw dropped. "You're my hero!" she exclaimed.

1. **From what point of view is the story told?**

_____

2. **Imagine you are Fastball Fran and that you are telling the story. On the back of this page, rewrite the story using the first-person point of view.**

Building Essential Writing Skills: Grade 3 © Scholastic Inc.

Organizer: The Talking Animal

Make up a story about a talking animal.
Write notes about your character, setting,
and plot on the organizer.

Character Traits

Name of Character

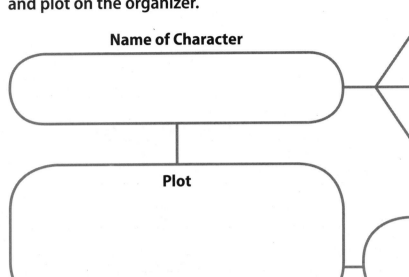

Plot

Setting

Events

1. _____

_____

2. _____

_____

3. _____

_____

4. _____

_____

Name: _____ Date: _____

Draft: The Talking Animal

Write the first draft of your story. Use your notes.

_____

_____

_____

_____

_____

_____

_____

_____

_____

_____

_____

Now check your work.

Words	Paragraphs	Punctuation and Grammar
☐ Use sequence words.	☐ Put events in logical order.	☐ Use capitalization and punctuation correctly.
☐ Spell words correctly.	☐ Use adjectives and adverbs for descriptive details.	☐ Punctuate any dialogue correctly.

Lesson 5: Pump Up Your Writing

Objective
Students will make their writing stronger and more interesting by making appropriate and concise word choices.

Standards
Demonstrate command of the conventions of standard English grammar and usage when writing.

What You Need
Copies of this packet for each student; whiteboard and markers

What to Do

1. Remind students that a noun is a person, place, or thing. A concrete noun is something that you can experience with one of your five senses. But some nouns cannot be experienced in a concrete way. Words such as *concept*, *freedom*, and *love* are **abstract nouns**. These nouns refer to an idea, feeling, experience, quality, or concept that you cannot see, hear, smell, touch, or taste. Display "That's So Abstract" (page 49) on the board and distribute copies to students. Have them complete the page to demonstrate their understanding of abstract nouns.

2. Tell students that some verbs (action words) are called **irregular verbs** because they do not follow a predictable spelling pattern when their tense changes. For example, the present-tense verb *go* becomes *went* when using the past tense. Similarly, the spelling of a singular irregular noun changes when it becomes a plural noun (for example, *tooth* and *teeth*). Display and/or distribute "An Irregular Camp" (page 50) and have students complete the activities.

3. Using each activity page in this packet, conduct a similar mini-lesson to focus on verb tenses, adjectives, adverbs, and word choice. Have students complete the pages, then review and discuss their responses as a class. Help them understand and correct any incorrect responses.

4. Have students take out and review their drafts from previous lessons. Ask them to reread their writing with a focus on word choice and grammar. Invite them to make corrections and changes to improve their writing.

A noun is a person, place, or thing. A concrete noun is something that you can experience with one of your five senses. An **abstract noun** is an idea, feeling, experience, quality, or concept that you cannot see, hear, smell, touch, or taste.

That's So Abstract

**Look at the words in the box.
These are all abstract nouns.**

> Did you know that the word *idea* is an abstract noun?

freedom	love	success	truth

1. Check each word below that is an abstract noun.

_____ **a.** peace   _____ **g.** car

_____ **b.** snow   _____ **h.** courage

_____ **c.** school   _____ **i.** loyalty

_____ **d.** liberty   _____ **j.** ball

_____ **e.** dream   _____ **k.** pride

_____ **f.** dog   _____ **l.** trust

2. Write a sentence. Use one concrete noun and one abstract noun from the list above.

_____

3. Write another sentence. Use an abstract noun in your sentence.

_____

Now circle the abstract nouns that you used in your sentences.

The spelling of an **irregular verb** changes when it goes from present to past tense. For example: *go/went, bring/brought, see/saw.*
The spelling of an **irregular noun** changes when it becomes plural. For example: *teeth/tooth, mouse/mice, goose/geese.*

An Irregular Camp

Read the passage Joe wrote.
Circle the correct verb in each verb pair.

I *(sit/sat)* quietly as Coach Callous barked orders at the new Superhero Super Camp campers. His loud, booming voice *(make/made)* me squirm. I really didn't *(understand/ understood)* why I was here. My mom *(think/thought)* it was a good idea, but I didn't. We *(are/were)* shouted out of our beds at 5 a.m. this morning. Then we had to *(stand/stood)* for hours while doctors tested us for possible superpowers. We finally got to sit, but we *(has/had)* to listen to a two-hour speech by Dr. Villain. When Dr. Villain finished, he *(tell/told)* us we could go. I hurried to the Dragon Lair and *(fight/fought)* dragons the rest of the afternoon. Now I'm sitting and listening again. I think I've *(hear/heard)* enough!

Now imagine you are fighting a dragon. Write about it. Use at least two irregular nouns from the box.

> children   feet   men   teeth   women

_____

_____

_____

_____

Building Essential Writing Skills: Grade 3 © Scholastic Inc.

Add -s to a present-tense verb when using it with a third-person singular noun: *The girl smiles. The girls smile.*
Add a -d or -ed for the past tense: *The girl smiled.*
For the simple future tense, use *will* before the verb: *The girl will smile.*

My Bird Feeder

Read the passage. Then complete the activities below.

Last week, my mom hooked a bird feeder on a branch outside my window. She remarked, "You will enjoy it. You will see all kinds of birds." Sure enough, on most days I see finches, cardinals, doves, and chickadees. Yesterday, I biked to the library for a bird book. I will find the many different birds at my feeder in the book. I will write them down in my journal. And if I listen closely, I will learn the birds by their song, too.

1. Draw a rectangle around the present-tense verbs in the paragraph.

2. Circle the past-tense verbs.

3. Underline the future tense verbs. (Hint: Look for the word *will*.)

4. Write a sentence using each verb tense shown.

Present: _____

Past: _____

Future: _____

An **adjective** describes a noun. An **adverb** describes a verb and often ends in –*ly*.

What Noise?

Read the story. Circle the correct adjective or adverb.

Ellie *(lazy/lazily)* daydreamed on the back porch. She didn't seem to hear her *(loud/loudly)* radio. She didn't hear the people screaming *(wild/wildly)* on a TV game show. And her computer played a *(noisy/noisily)* action movie. Ellie just kept *(peaceful/peacefully)* dreaming. Little did she know that a storm was *(quick/quickly)* approaching. Won't Ellie be surprised if the storm knocks out the electricity, and all the noise around her is *(sudden/suddenly)* silenced!

Now write a story about the approaching storm. Use adjectives and adverbs in your sentences.

_____

_____

_____

_____

_____

Building Essential Writing Skills: Grade 3 © Scholastic Inc.

Some words have almost the same meaning, but there are small, important differences. For example, *chilly*, *cold*, and *freezing* all have similar meanings, but you would choose *freezing* to describe a really cold day because it has the strongest meaning.

The Storm

A storm is approaching a town. Describe the scene by completing each sentence. Choose the word that has the stronger meaning.

1. It will be a _____ night with high winds and lightning.   **rainy   stormy**

2. I already see _____, dark clouds forming.   **heavy   big**

3. Parents _____ home to make sure everyone was safe.   **ran   rushed**

4. Rain _____ out of the sky for hours.   **fell   poured**

5. Overnight, several trees _____ to the ground in the park.   **crashed   dropped**

6. The next day, the sun _____ in the clear sky.   **glowed   blazed**

It's a nice day.

It's a gorgeous day.

Choose specific words with precise meanings to make your writing lively and interesting.

Superheroes Needed!

Read this ad. Complete each sentence with the most precise word. Write that word on the line.

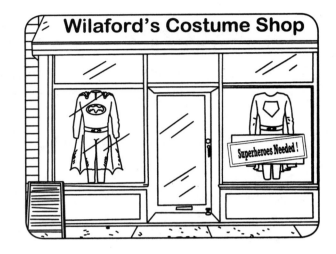

Wilaford's Costume Shop

Superheroes Needed!

(1) We do not need you to leap tall buildings

in a single _____

(bound/jump), because we already have

a superhero for that. (2) We also have a superhero

who can _____ *(make/spin)* a spider web. (3) And one who can

run at _____ *(fast/record)* speeds. (4) We need new superheroes

to _____ *(battle/fix)* today's problems.

Replace the underlined word in each sentence below with a more precise word. Write your word choice on the line. Use a word from the box.

> keen   create   sketch   bursting   wonderful

(5) Are you <u>filled</u> with ideas?   _____

(6) Can you <u>draw</u> figures well?   _____

(7) Do you have a <u>strong</u> sense of color and fashion?   _____

(8) Then come on down to Wilaford's
Weird and <u>Cool</u> Costume Shop.   _____

(9) Help us <u>make</u> the next superhero sensation!   _____

Building Essential Writing Skills: Grade 3 © Scholastic Inc.

Lesson 6: Revising and Editing

Objective

Students will make corrections and revisions to improve their writing, then produce a final copy.

Standards

• Develop and strengthen writing as needed by revising and editing.
• Produce and publish different types of writing independently and in collaboration with peers.

What You Need

Copies of this packet for each student; whiteboard and markers

What to Do

1. Display "And They're Off …" (page 56) on the board and distribute copies to students. Point out the editing marks and explain what each one means. Write a few sentences on the board and demonstrate how to use the different marks. Then have students edit the passage on their copy of the page. When finished, invite volunteers to come to the board and mark the mistakes in the passage. Ask students to check their work as each mistake is marked on the board. Finally, have them complete the rest of the page. For additional reinforcement, distribute "Helpful Weather Reports" (page 57) for students to complete.

2. Use "A Duck-Billed Platypus" (page 58) and "All About Autumn" (page 59) to give students practice in revising sentences by expanding or combining them, or by adding details. When finished, review the changes they made to the sentences and discuss how the changes make the passages more interesting and easier to understand.

3. Display "A Hot, Dry Place" (page 60) on the board. Distribute copies to students. Explain that when sentences in a paragraph are properly sequenced, the text flows and is easier for the reader to understand. Have students complete the page, then review it as a class. Discuss why some sentences work better in one place than in another in the paragraph.

4. Have students take out their drafts from previous lessons. Invite them to correct and revise the text as needed and write a final draft on a copy of the writing template (page 61).

To **revise** your writing, add words or take out words. Check your sentences for correct spelling, end punctuation, and capital letters. Use editing marks to help with your revisions.

And They're Off . . .

∧ **Add**	ℓ **Take Out**	/ **Small Letter**
⊙ **Period**	≡ **Capital Letter**	⬭ **Spelling Error**

Sample: always revise ≡ Edit ℓ your ∧*and* your ∧*work* ⬭worck⊙

Review the editing marks above. Then revise the following passage using the editing marks.

(1) One of the oldest and fast sports in America is horse racing! (2) The Kentucky Derby is the best because takes only about two minutes for horses to finish. (3) It also has the most intresting history. (4) It was founded by Meriwether Lewis Clark, Jr (5) He was the grandson of William Clark, the famous explorer. (6) Meriwether learned about horse racing in england. (7) He started the Louisville Jockey club. (8) His uncles, John And Henry Churchill, owned lots and lots of property in Kentucky. (9) In 1875, some 10,000 people came to a race track owned by the Churchill family. (10) They watched fifteen horses line up; then they were off and running!

1. Combine sentences 4 and 5 into one sentence.

_____

_____

2. What change could be made in sentence 10?
  a. Change *watched* to *watch*.
  b. Change *horses* to *jockeys*.
  c. Change *they* to *the horses* in the second part of the sentence.

Building Essential Writing Skills: Grade 3 © Scholastic Inc.

Proofread your final draft by checking for mistakes in spelling, capitalization, and punctuation.

Helpful Weather Reports

Read the draft about weather reports. Find the seven spelling, capitalization, and punctuation mistakes. Mark them with editing marks.

Did you know that weather reports tell us a lot of good information? We can see on maps where bad weather is happening. This lets us no if it is moving toward us. On a monday, weather reports can tell us if it will rane on Saturday. This is called a weather forecast weather experts study where kool and warm air is. They also find out what the pressure of the air is. They record the speed and direction of winds, and where clouds are. All of this lets us make the rite plans for the weekend.

Rewrite each sentence that has a mistake.

_____

_____

_____

_____

_____

_____

Now proofread and edit a draft of a text you've written. Then rewrite your text on another sheet of paper.

When revising your draft, look for ways to include a variety of sentence types. For example, add words to expand a sentence, or combine two sentences to make a compound sentence.

A Duck-Billed Platypus

Read Gary's draft about his visit to the zoo.

My family took a trip to the Melbourne Zoo today. I saw a duck-billed platypus! I stared at it for a long time. It's the weirdest-looking animal I've ever seen. It has a bill like a duck. It doesn't quack. The platypus has a flat tail. It has fur like a beaver. The fur traps air. This helps the platypus stay afloat in water. Its front paws are webbed. They help it swim in the water. It swims along the bottom like a catfish. The platypus eats whatever it can scoop up with its bill. Its eyes stay closed when it's underwater.

Now look at ways some of the sentences can be combined. Write a word to link each of the sentences below. Use words from the box. (Hint: Use each word only once.)

> and   because   but   since   so

1. I stared at it for a long time, _____ it's the weirdest-looking animal I've ever seen.

2. It has a bill like a duck, _____ it doesn't quack.

3. The platypus has a flat tail, _____ it has fur like a beaver.

4. Its front paws are webbed, _____ they help it swim in the water.

5. The platypus eats whatever it can scoop up with its bill, _____ its eyes stay closed when it's underwater.

Look at sentence 3 above. Which words can you remove to make the sentence flow better? Write your new sentence.

_____

Now look for ways to improve sentences in a draft of a text you've written.
Then rewrite your text on another sheet of paper.

Building Essential Writing Skills: Grade 3 © Scholastic Inc.

Adding a word or phrase can provide more detail and help make your writing more descriptive.

All About Autumn

Read the passage.

When summer turns to autumn, ^ changes happen. With cooler temperatures and less sunlight, tree leaves stop making food. This changes their color ^. Squirrels scamper around ^. They hide their food underground ^. It will be ready for them when there is less food in the winter. Birds migrate ^ to warmer winter homes. Nature is ^ when the weather changes in autumn.

Some sentences have the editing mark for Add (^). These are places where a word or phrase can be added to make the sentence more interesting. Which is the best word or phrase below to add to each sentence above? Write that number in the circle above the Add (^) mark.

1. collecting acorns and other nuts

2. in great flocks

3. quite busy

4. special

5. and inside hollow trees

6. from green to many shades of orange, red, yellow, and purple

Read the passage to a partner. Use the added words and phrases in the sentences as you read. You can also rewrite the text with the revisions on another sheet of paper.

Name: _____   Date: _____

> When you complete a draft, reread it to make sure the text makes sense and that sentences are in a logical order.

A Hot, Dry Place

Read the passage. Then complete the activities below.

(1) The hottest, driest place in the United States is Death Valley, California. (2) It only rains about 2 inches all year. (3) In spite of the extreme conditions, plenty of plants and animals survive in the dry heat of Death Valley. (4) In July, the average high temperature is 117 degrees. (5) Wildflowers grow in the spring. (6) With the scorching heat, there's a surprising amount of life in Death Valley! (7) Roadrunners, jackrabbits, rattlesnakes, kangaroo rats, and even a species of fish live there all year.

1. Read sentence 4. Where can this sentence be moved to help the text flow better?

    a. after sentence 7

    b. before sentence 1

    c. between sentences 5 and 6

    d. between sentences 1 and 2

2. Which sentence should be moved to the end of the passage to use as the conclusion?

    a. sentence 5

    b. sentence 3

    c. sentence 6

    d. sentence 2

Now read the passage to a partner. Read the sentences in an order that makes sense. You can rewrite the text with the revisions of the sentence order. Use another sheet of paper.

Building Essential Writing Skills: Grade 3 © Scholastic Inc.

Name: _____   Date: _____

Title: _____

_____

_____

_____

_____

_____

_____

_____

_____

_____

_____

_____

_____

_____

Answer Key

1. (A rabbit)
2. the rabbit
3. sprang
4. (the rabbit) stopped
5. Sentences will vary.

p. 9
1. Tell me why.
2. You must be joking!
3. It's special because it can't fly?
4. d

p. 10
1. Sunshine State, Arizona's
2. United States
3. Yuma, Arizona
4. none
5. June
6. St. Petersburg, Florida
7. February, March
8. none

p. 11
1. My friend Enrique visited Springfield Safari Park last week. Animals from Africa roam freely around the park.
2. Enrique drove his car through the park. He said an ostrich stuck its head into the sunroof!
3. A zebra, llama, and warthog also came right up to his car. Enrique enjoyed seeing so many animals up close.
4. Would you like to visit a safari park? What animals would you hope to see?

p. 12
1. "What's the matter?" asked Yadier.
2. "I'm not sure," replied Jasper.
3. "Tingly, like your foot is asleep?"
4. "No, tingly like my feet are ready to run 200 miles a minute."
5. "Wow! That's a pretty good tingle," said Yadier.

p. 13
is, is, falls, are, has, plunge, is, develop, stays
1. it
2. they
3. she
4. they

p. 14
1–3. Sentences will vary.

p. 15
1. the lightning struck 8 miles away; b
2. the lightning is about 6 miles away; c

p. 16
1. They have an important job.
2. They must do it safely.
3. They pass information on to weather services, and these services pass it on to you.
4. Storm chasers may see a tornado and follow its path, but they don't want to be *in* the tornado's path.

p. 18
1. b
2. The gray wolf needs to be rescued again. Introductions will vary.

p. 19
1. Like lightning and tornadoes, (hail can be a dangerous part of a thunderstorm.)
2. b
3. Introductions will vary.

p. 20
1. a
2. I think my dog is smarter than my sister. Conclusions will vary.

p. 21
1. Sample answer: What's good and bad about humidity
2. Conclusions will vary.
3. Conclusions will vary.

p. 22
Sometimes the ocean can be foamy like a bubble bath.
(It might be fun to swim in an ocean-size bathtub of foam, but it won't make you clean!)
1. Sample answer: How sea foam forms
2. Answers will vary.

p. 23
2, 5, 3, 1, 4
Conclusions will vary.

p. 25
1. c
2. Answers will vary.
3. Answers will vary.

p. 26
1. c
2. Animals belong in the wild.
3. Answers will vary.

p. 27
1. Reasons will vary.
2. c
3. Sentences will vary for each reason.

p. 28
1. Storms at Sea
2. Wettest Places in the World
3. a

p. 29
1. b
2. Questions will vary.
3. Questions will vary.

p. 30
1. d
2. Questions will vary.
3. Responses will vary.

p. 31
1. dictionary
2. encyclopedia
3. weather website
4. atlas

p. 32
1. Answers will vary.
2. Answers will vary.
3. Answers will vary.

p. 33
Answers will vary for all sections of the organizer.

p. 34
3, 5, 1, 4, 6, 2
1. First, Finally, Then, From then on, One day
2. Answers will vary.

p. 36
1. b
2. c
3. a
Drafts will vary.

p. 37
1. The nickname for our school sports team should be Gazelles. If our team is fast and smart, and our players are good sports, we will have many championship seasons.
2. Sample answer: Gazelles are fast, smart, and good sports.
3. c

p. 40
1. If you've ever seen a whirl of dust rising in the air, it may have been a dust devil. c
2. Answers will vary.

p. 43
1. Norman Haskin; answers will vary.
2. Norman's backyard in Headwind, Kansas; answers will vary.
3. Answers will vary.

p. 44
Stories will vary.

p. 45
1. third person
2. I had just completed my 384th no-hitter. As I signed autographs outside the stadium, an elderly woman came up and congratulated me. "That was an excellent game today," she said.
   "Thanks," I mumbled without looking up.
   "I used to pitch, too," added the woman.
   "Really?" I said disbelievingly.
   "Yes," replied the woman. "Want to see?"
   I handed the woman a ball, then walked several feet away. When I held up my mitt, the elderly woman threw a fastball, right in the strike zone!
   "Wow!" I remarked, as I jogged back to the woman. "You're amazing!"
   "Thank you," replied the woman. "I used to pitch for the All-American Girls Professional Baseball League. My name is Jean Faut."
   My jaw dropped. "You're my hero!" I exclaimed.

p. 49
1. a, d, e, h, i, k, l
2. Sentences will vary.
3. Sentences will vary.
Students should circle the abstract nouns in their sentences.

p. 50

sat, made, understand, thought, were, stand, had, told, fought, heard

Answers will vary.

p. 51

1. see, listen
2. hooked, remarked, biked
3. will enjoy, will see, will find, will write, will learn
4. Sentences will vary.

p. 52

lazily, loud, wildly, noisy, peacefully, quickly, suddenly

Stories will vary.

p. 53

1. stormy
2. heavy
3. rushed
4. poured
5. crashed
6. blazed

p. 54

1. bound
2. spin
3. record
4. battle
5. bursting
6. sketch
7. keen
8. wonderful
9. create

p. 56

(1) One of the oldest and ~~fast~~ *fastest* sports in America is horse racing! (2) The Kentucky Derby is the best because *it* takes only about two minutes for horses to finish, and it has the most ~~intresting~~ *interesting* history. (3) It was founded by Meriwether Lewis Clark, Jr. (4) He was the grandson of William Clark, the famous explorer. (5) Meriwether learned about horse racing in england. (6) He started the Louisville Jockey club. (7) His uncles, John And Henry Churchill, owned lots and lots of property in Kentucky. (8) In 1875, some 10,000 people came to a race track owned by the Churchill family. (9) They watched fifteen horses line up; then they were off and running!

1. It was founded by Meriwether Lewis Clark, Jr., who was the grandson of William Clark, the famous explorer.
2. c

p. 57

Students should rewrite the following sentences:

This lets us know if it is moving toward us.

On a Monday, weather reports can tell us if it will rain on Saturday.

This is called a weather forecast.

Weather experts study where cool and warm air is.

All of this lets us make the right plans for the weekend.

p. 58

1. because
2. but
3. and
4. so
5. since

Sample answer: The platypus has a flat tail and fur like a beaver.

p. 59

4, 6, 1, 5, 2, 3

p. 60

1. d
2. c